Samac

Step-by-Step Guide To Elevate Your
Consciousness and Spirituality with Samadhi

Lena Lind & Peter Harris

TABLE OF CONTENTS

CHAPTER 1
SAMADHI - STATE OF ONE-NESS

Samadhi is the eighth step of yoga. The great Sage Gheranda says, "There is no yoga without Samadhi. None is so fortunate as the person who attains samadhi. Samadhi can be attained by devotedly serving the guru and securing his grace."1in this statement an important doctrine, full of truth, is laid down. Since in samadhi one has to achieve the constraint of the mind by stopping its fluctuations, the sage has said that there cannot be yoga without Samadhi.

The end product of any yoga can only be this. It matters little by what name we call it. Another doctrine laid out in the above statement is that the state of samadhi is not attainable without the grace of a realized guru. Only a lighted candle can light an unlighted one. The truth of this cannot be negated simply because some inexperienced people do not agree with it.

In Hatha Yoga Pradipika it is said, "As salt dissolves in water, so the mind dissolves into the soul and becomes one with it. The unity of soul and mind is called Samadhi."Yajnavalkya says, "The union of jivatman (soul) with paramatman (God) is known as Samadhi. The state in which the jivatman establishes itself in the paramatman is the state of Samadhi."Raja Yoga, unmani, manomani, amaratva, laya, tattva, sunyasunya, paramapada,amanaska, advaita, niralamba, niranjana, jivanamukti, sahajavastha, turyavastha – all these are other words for Samadhi.

Sage Patanjali says, "That stage of meditation in which one realizes the goal, and forms dissolve from the mind, is the state of Samadhi."After intense practice, when meditation is no longer meditation, but becomes identified with or merged into the goal, this is called Samadhi.

In speaking of Samadhi we are referring to the supreme states of human consciousness when, beyond the petty ego, an individual occasionally is released into the universal consciousness beyond, to taste the Reality which exists in the patterned beauty of the infinite life in which we are a part and to which we are usually blind. These expansions of consciousness are rare but well known enough by account, to allow us to accept that we also have a potential to experience the same.

To help us realize these ecstatic states beyond the normal range of human thought and emotion, the system of Yoga has been designed. But it is not only for the individual's experience alone, as it must be translated into some expression which allows others to share, if only a droplet, or for a moment, that reflected experience of spiritual Realization when all sense of separation vanishes, and life seems as One.

It must be remembered that knowing something with the mind and realizing it are two different experiences. Any form of realization can be compared with a little light going on in one's consciousness. This occurs together with new comprehension and insight. So realization on any level is a very special state and may occur infrequently, but when it comes, makes a lasting impression.

Spiritual Realization is similar but magnified many times, as anticipated when the focus is upon God, and it produces an inner excitement of one's being. One feels to have suddenly known the Reality of the Universe and of the part each life plays in the great drama of the Cosmos. It represents the climax in the inner meditative and expansive experiencing of the yogi.

Samadhi is the experiencing of the heavenly states, beyond normal range of human life and results in keener perceptions, fresh perspectives or a greater comprehension that requires old conclusions to be reviewed and seen in a new light. It is through human realizations that entirely new discoveries are made and it is through spiritual realizations that the truths of the spiritual Realities become known.

All who experience it are left with a memory of having tasted a rare and supreme joy beyond previously known conditions of human happiness - a tantalizing taste of heaven!

TOTAL CONCENTRATION (SAMADHI) OF MIND

A true Yogi (practitioner) is one who has acquired self-knowledge and through continuous practice and detachment has been able to rest in true self, so firmly that he seldom slips down from it. Samadhi is the state where one realizes the true self or soul. When true self is realized everything is realized.

There are three kinds of Samadhi –

- Samprajnata (conscious),
- Asamprajnata (supraconscious) and
- Jada (inert).

Let us first see what Samprajnata Samadhi is. Patanjali describes - Samprajnata is achieved by following argument (vitarka), analysis (vichara), bliss (ananda) and egoism (asmita).

When a Yogi turns away from all those things that are either seen or heard of, he begins to think about himself, like - who am I; why I am here; what to do here; what this world(samsara) is; who is God and where does He lives. In this way many arguments (vitarka) appear in his mind. In order to know the truth he reads scriptures, listens to wise people and starts analyzing (vichara) what he learnt. A true analyst always ends up with the truth. Upanishads have glorified human beings and soul (atman). Atman has been described as Brahman, the ultimate reality.

So after right analysis when a Yogi finds out that he himself is that glorified super being, he feels the bliss (ananda). This develops egoism (asmita) in him, as there is none greater than him. In this way and with these thoughts a Yogi enters into Samadhi and realizes himself. This is the Samprajnata (conscious) Samadhi.

Then comes the Asamprajnata (supracoscious) Samadhi. When a Yogi enters into Samadhi regularly he becomes so much adept in this practice that he no longer thinks about practice, detachment or true self. All of these become part and parcel of his body and mind. Whenever he wishes he enters into Samadhi. Patanjali describes Asamprajnata Samadhi as - the state where practice for controlling of thoughts remains merely as memory, becomes Asamprajnata Samadhi which is other than the Samprajnata Samadhi. In this state, thoughts, controlling of thoughts, practice and detachment; all these things remain as memory or impression. One only feels the bliss of true self. This state cannot be described adequately.

Then let us see what Jada (inert) Samadhi is. In both the Samprajnata and Asamprajnata Samadhi consciousness is never lost. These are such sleeping states where one is waking and fully conscious. A conscious being should not try to become unconscious at any state. However many people try to enter into Samadhi unconsciously. They remain unconscious for several hours/days. This is Jada (inert) Samadhi. Patanjali describes - the state of unconsciousness and disappearing into the material world is due to the act of inertness.

Unconsciousness is the state where one is not aware of one's own body, mind or self. It is like entering into a comatic state. One disappears into material world and becomes as good as or as bad as matter. So instead of trying to become a material thing one should try to become more conscious, gracious, blissful and intelligent. Unconsciousness is a disease in Samadhi.

One who thinks that soul is separate from and inferior to God, one cannot realize one's true self and enter into Samadhi. Only a Yogi who knows that soul is not different from God, may enter into Samadhi. For this Patanjali instructs - by bearing (pranidhan) God (Ishvara) in oneself. One should bear God in one's heart of deeper mind. For most people it may seem highly improbable, because how God may be carried in one's heart. For this Patanjali describes who God Is.

Any human being (purushavishesh) who has separated himself from those evil thoughts which generate such fruits of action that give pain is God (Ishvara). So one is God who has dispelled all evil thoughts from the mind. Evil thoughts may be controlled when one realizes that soul is God and when one bears Godliness qualities in himself. By this he transforms himself from a mere mortal being to God.

Krishna, Buddha, Jesus and Mohammad were all God. They had imbibed all those divine attributes which people believe to exist in God.

All these divine attributes emanates from soul (atman) for this the aim of Yoga is to realize true self

HOW TO EXPERIENCE THE BLISS OF SAMADHI

Are you ready for a powerful spiritual experience that will transform your entire life? Samadhi is an ancient Sanskrit word that literally means "the bliss from transcending the mind". Samadhi is a state of perfect "clear seeing" that recognizes the Divine within yourself, in everything around you, and in every person you meet.

The state of Samadhi is a profound spiritual experience where you explore deep joy, expansive feelings of lightness, love, connection to the Divine and enlightenment. It is unique from other paths on the spiritual quest in that it goes directly to the Source of pure consciousness and remains there. Samadhi is the highest spiritual experience you can have.

It opens you up to your most enlightened self who is free from worry, fear and any attachment to this world. One who is living their life in Samadhi Consciousness feels only love, oneness, and peace within every experience they have. When you receive your first taste of Samadhi there is a deep knowing that all is one, and that "oneness" is at the core of which you are.

Enlightenment is not about imagining figures of light, But of making the darkness conscious!

In Samadhi, there is such a tremendous feeling of bliss because there is truly no inner judge or discriminatory mind present. There may be thoughts that pass through the mind, yet you are no longer clinging onto them. One who has entered the state of Samadhi discovers a deep personal, intimate merging with the Divine Being within themselves, and as well within everyone they meet. The ego within others and yourself is easily seen and transcended in Samadhi Consciousness. You are truly unified, connected, and at peace with everyone in the Universe on every level.

You experience an eternally expanding realization that this world and your ego is not real, and that the real you (the soul, spirit and divine essence) is who you truly are and will never die. To reach Samadhi, it takes a profound state of constant deep surrender to the Divine. By relaxing into each and every experience you'll discover the pure consciousness that is not attached to any thought, feeling, or idea. By surrendering to this consciousness you will eventually arrive at a state of bliss.

You wander restlessly from forest to forest while the Reality is within your own dwelling. The Truth is here! Until you have found God in your own Soul, the whole world will seem meaningless to you.

Life is truly amazing in Samadhi consciousness. Anything is truly possible in this divine spiritually enlightened connection when we realize that WE ARE ONE with the Universe. You have the power to create. Your power is so strong that whatever you believe comes true.

Samadhi can happen to anyone who is devoted to finding the Truth of who they really are. The divine spiritual essence is within you now in this moment. The mind however can be very addicted to patterns of seeing yourself and the world, and may require the focus of a Guru, spiritual teacher, and/or deep inner devotion to self-inquiry to unravel itself and find this permanent state of freedom.

The untrained mind is like a wild caged animal that is unable to trust, relax and remain at peace for even 10 seconds. In Samadhi consciousness the mind is trained to be here now, so there is no mind chatter. Your mind is completely at ease with life, fully in the present moment, and truly free from worry and concern. Problems from your past become illusory issues which you realize you were always free from the appearance of their grasp.

Don't ask yourself what the world needs; ask yourself what makes you come alive! And then go and do that. Because what the world needs is people who are truly alive. ~ Harold Whitman

In Samadhi consciousness you are so completely free, and unlimited that all things are possible to you. It's not just that they "seem" possible, they ARE possible. Your mind-body's vibration is so high that your ability to manifest is truly unstoppable. The wildest thing is that this ever-expanding state of bliss is available within you right now.

If you are open to exploring what this magical state is like, the guided meditation below will take you on a journey to drop through the mind chatter so that you may get a taste of this highest state of consciousness.

CHAPTER 2
THE JOURNEY TO
ENLIGHTENMENT

There are two categories of what is called enlightenment. First, there is enlightenment that comes from the mind. This includes enlightenment of the mental body where people receive a certain amount of illumination that happens through the mind, and it also includes the many ideas of enlightenment" which are Illusions of enlightenment. The word "enlightenment" is used very loosely today to apply to a lot of different spiritual practices and mental states" So, there are many ideas about enlightenment, and even more ideas about the illusions of enlightenment.

The second aspect to enlightenment is of the heart. It is talked about considerably in the Buddhic, Vedantic and Sufi paths, and to a far lesser extent in other paths. Enlightenment of the heart is a different focus from that of the mind, and, in my view, enlightenment of the mind is incomplete without the enlightenment of the heart.

In order to bring our soul into the physical dimension, we have been clothed in a garment which can live in this degree of density. This garment is our personality which is composed of physical, emotional, mental, and etheric bodies. What happens in the process of life experiences is that our soul becomes caught in the personality, which, in turn, gets caught in the pain and other illusions that are characteristic of the physical dimension. The experiences in this plane which were supposed to be of love, beauty, and fulfillment have become distorted into deep experiences of limitations and the deepest limitations are pain, suffering and disease.

THE CHALLENGE

Every time someone throws their emotions at you it challenges you to see if you can maintain the love within you that is the core essence of your being, in spite of what the other person's emotional upset. If your lover or boss comes in screaming at you, can you hold the love? If we want to match the love quality of God, we must do the same for others. If you get hooked by the other person's emotions, you lose your center and your love, and become entangled with like emotions. This further encases you in the illusions of the lower emotions. Ask yourself why you fell into this trap? Why did you forget? Why did you lose yourself? Go inside yourself and purify that place so you don't forget the next time it happens.

To progress on the enlightened path you must become equal-minded or neutral unaffected by victory or defeat, profit or loss, joy or sorrow, hot or cold, honor or dishonor, or any other pairs of opposites. When you are equal-minded you will experience joy and feelings of love and satisfaction regardless of outer circumstances. When you reach this state, others can no longer hook you with their emotions or illusions.

This is a very high way to live, and brings great freedom with it. If you are not living with that freedom, you are like a cork floating on water in a storm" being pushed around by the projections of everyone around you" letting their illusions rule and create your reality. If you live this way, you are letting the blind leading the blind" letting another person's illusions create deeper illusions, and you both live in a state of limitation and pain. Be free. When someone throws something at you, you recognize it as an illusion, and say, "I love you, but I'm not interested in losing my love and leaving my heart."

Somehow humanity has lost track of its Divine essence and became lost in personalities and living according to the desires of the personalities. We are all trying to get out of the limitations we have become ensnared with, and so we pursue multiple paths to relieve the suffering.

What if we were to orient our efforts totally to seeking God and God only? Not God as a concept, not God as a being judging us, but to the Divine truth and intelligence that lives within us all. And what if we were to commit ourselves totally and completely to that? What if we were willing to clear the veils of illusion that cover our hearts from the full experience of our Divinity?

Most are confused by their emotions, and so they live in mental worlds of constant thinking, plotting, reasoning, wondering, analyzing, and

17

scheming. But, remember, the mind creates illusions, and that is all it can ever create. The mind creates illusions about who and what you are, and they run very wide and deep. Each person's illusions are then projected on others, and every illusion has a core of followers. So, in life you find a confusing choice of options to distract you from your goal. If you, yourself, live in illusions and not your Divinity, you will be easily distracted by the philosophies and projections of others which can only manifest lack, limitation, pain, and disease.

Your energy field is formed by your thoughts, and your thoughts create energy patterns in your subtle bodies. These energy patterns create and attract conditions and situations based on the character and quality of those thoughts. Those patterns also coalesce into the physical body itself. Depending on the nature of those thoughts a person's life and health will eventually reflect the quality of the thoughts.

THE PSYCHOLOGY OF ENLIGHTENMENT

On the stages of enlightenment and why enlightenment is the only unique psychological experience and the only factor that makes a person great. There is absolutely no substantial research data in psychology to suggest that enlightenment is a real psychological process. Very little research has been done on the process of enlightenment and enlightenment is generally considered as some sort of abstract elevated thinking that provides a spiritual connection between a human being and the ultimate reality. Enlightenment is often considered wisdom and is found among the seekers of truth, wisdom or ultimate reality.

The ordinary dictionary definition of enlightenment is that it is wisdom, insight, self-awareness, self-realization or the ultimate grasp or understanding of higher knowledge. Enlightenment may also indicate reason and individualism according to an 18th century Western philosophical movement. In this discussion, we will consider the personal experience of enlightenment.

Enlightenment is knowledge through one's own self awareness, it is knowledge through the senses and not based on study or learning. Enlightenment is thus 'inner knowledge' or a person's basic innate understanding of how the Universe works. It is a never-ending debate whether enlightenment finally depends on innate knowledge or formal education. An uneducated man can be highly enlightened as he gains knowledge from his environment.

He learns about the falling leaves, changing seasons, the flow of the river, the sounds of the birds or the direction of the winds. Even if this man living in a natural environment never reads a book, he can become enlightened with the knowledge of the universe if he develops his own powers of thinking by observing the environment. If you've read books like Siddhartha or the Alchemist or even other old stories and spiritual scriptures you probably understand that in ancient times, people used their knowledge of the environment, to gain an insight into the workings of the universe.

Enlightened individuals have heightened sense awareness, they are self aware, acutely observant, more perceptive, more intuitive about the future, they have keen psychological understanding, can pick up people's motives rather easily and can quickly adapt to the environment. They are also extremely curious, and take in and manage a large amount of information, so every internal and external event becomes a learning experience.

If you are still thinking that enlightenment is some sort of abstract, undefined wisdom or power of insight in individuals that is only partially correct. Enlightenment is also a definite psychological process. Not everyone who is knowledgeable can be considered enlightened because not everyone experiences this very specific process of enlightenment.

When we think about enlightenment, the first person that comes to mind is the Buddha. Buddha's life story is clearly about his journey from materialistic possessions to that of spiritual seeking and when he found enlightenment under a Peepal tree, he transformed from Gautama the king, to Buddha, the Enlightened one. What Buddha experienced is spiritual Enlightenment and this sort of enlightenment is a specific psychological process. The "Buddha syndrome "as I would call it, is not an experience uniquely felt by the Buddha.

It is a real psychological experience felt by every spiritual or scientific seeker. There are seven distinct stages of enlightenment and every spiritual seeker or enlightened individual, whether a saint or a scientist goes through exactly the same stages and the emotional, spiritual or intellectual experience of enlightenment is also exactly the same.

Thus enlightenment is actually a very objective and definable spiritual, intellectual and emotional experience. But psychologists have not been able to define it or study it because this is a rare phenomenon; it does not happen to everyone.

The process of spiritual Enlightenment is not a gradual one. It is a very sudden earth-shattering experience. It lasts for a few seconds or minutes and like a sudden bolt of lightning it has a major impact on the individual's entire being. People who have experienced this sort of enlightenment felt they were momentarily immersed in a universe that connects to their soul and they felt their souls for the first time in their lives or they felt they were drowning in an immensely powerful light.

You must have read about out of the world or out of the body experiences and enlightenment actually is both. During those few seconds of intense psychological experience, you are suddenly able to get out of the body and out of this world and you are able to observe your body and this universe from an outsider's perspective. Yet, strangely you also feel connected to this Universe in a very intimate way, as if the whole universe is within you or somehow connected to you.

Anyone who has gone through this experience will be so completely shaken that it takes a while to recover. Some may lose their minds temporarily and it becomes a very personal experience that they will never forget.

Enlightenment is one special moment in your life when you connect directly with the higher power or the cosmic force of the Universe and you actually merge with this Universal power and feel the same power within you.

This is what Buddha felt; this is what many spiritual seekers, scientists, writers and artists feel when they find enlightenment. They feel a connection with the universe, they feel a connection with their souls, an all consuming light around them and they feel immense power and a deep knowledge about the Universe.

The specific process of enlightenment comprises of:

1. An intense light in which the individual feels completely immersed,

2. An intense personal and intimate connection with the Universe,

3. A sudden deep knowledge about the Universe, the individual can almost see the past and the future,

4. An undefinable power like they have the entire Universe within themselves and 5. A nerve-racking connection with their own souls or being.

This sudden experience of connection with the soul is very frightening; it shakes one's very existence as they may have never believed in a soul or a cosmic force before the specific experience of enlightenment. But this is a very real experience. It has happened to Buddha, it has happened to Einstein and to millions of others who have seen it and felt it.

Enlightenment usually happens rather early in life, usually in early twenties. It throws the individual straight into an existential crisis as he begins to question his purpose, his existence, his value, his life and the world around him. He questions his faith, his family, the meaning of his identity. He may not relate to his tiny spatio-temporal identity anymore, because he has felt limitlessness and what it feels to live as a soul, from the beginning until the end of time and space.

I know you may feel this is just a spiritual experience you cannot relate to because you are an atheist or that all spiritual books have similar points. But, I am not talking about God. Spiritual Enlightenment has nothing to do with our traditional concepts of God or religion. It is a psychological, emotional and intellectual experience with spiritual dimensions. It is almost like falling in love with the Universe and feeling a deep connection with your own inner being.

THE STAGES OF ENLIGHTENMENT ARE AS FOLLOWS

1. Emotional crisis, including angst, depression, restlessness. Enlightenment always begins with an emotional turmoil or crisis.

2. Intellectual crisis, when the individual seeks purpose, goal and meaning in life. The individual tries to rationalize the emotions intellectually.

3. Heightened sensibilities, sensitivity and curiosity. The individual is highly sensitive and becomes more open or receptive at this stage

4. Sudden realization, a life-changing experience of connection with the Universe and soul or cosmic power. This is the sudden moment of extreme light, knowledge and power.

5. Existential crisis, often marked by temporary mental illness, exhaustion, near starvation and insomnia. Following the earth shattering experience of enlightenment, the individual might become temporarily ill or feel extremely tired and may try to move away from home or immediate family

6. Gaining knowledge through intense periods of study of sciences, scriptures, religions, history, arts or philosophy. This is the stage of finally coming to terms with the experience and the need to understand it better.

7. Self-realization, inner peace and identification of one's purpose and meaning in life. A deep love for humanity and the universe, a sense of calm, heightened intuition and a strong drive and sense of mission.

STEPS TO BECOME ENLIGHTENED

If you want to become enlightened, there are certain things that are pretty much necessary to follow in order for you to really move deep into the enlightened state. Regardless of your spiritual path or beliefs, if you follow these 5 steps to become enlightened, you will be well on your way.

1.The first step to become enlightened is shaktipat. Also known as Kundalini Shakti, Deeksha or Grace, shaktipat is the spiritual energy that awakens you to enlightenment.

Although spiritual practice and meditation is important if you want to become enlightened, ultimately it is this spiritual energy that awakens you to enlightenment. When this Shaktipat becomes awakened in you, you may feel this energy as bliss, or love or peace. Simply by allowing your attention to remain in that bliss, the Shakti purifies your energy channels and awakens you into your natural enlightened state.

The main way you receive shaktipat is through an enlightened master, one who has reached such a high state of enlightenment that they radiate shaktipat. Just by sitting with them, this spiritual energy is awakened in you and enlightenment happens.

But there is also a way you can receive shaktipat through sound which we will talk about at the end of this write up.

2. The second step in becoming enlightened is purification. Proper diet and exercise is most important. You have to bring you body into a very balanced and pure state. If you are drinking alcohol, taking drugs, eating junk food, your body will be busy fighting all of these toxins and will remain unbalanced. You want to eat pure foods, lots of fresh fruit and vegetables, food that nurtures the body and mind.

3.The third step to become enlightened is spiritual practice. Some form of meditation is usually the main practice, but prana (breathing) exercises, chanting, yoga can also be quite beneficial. It is important to keep an open mind, to try the different spiritual practices that are talked about by various enlightened teachers and see what works for you.

4.The fourth step to become enlightened is discipline: to find the spiritual practices that you find beneficial and do them every day. It helps to do them at the same time every day also. I like to get up early, go for a run, do yoga, prana exercises, puja and chanting and then meditate before I do anything else. And then I meditate again before dinner and again before I go to bed.

You should follow what works for you, but keeping a disciplined routine builds the energy. If you want to become enlightened it is important to build this energy and not let yourself fall into laziness and distractions. In my experience the idea of just "doing whatever you feel like doing" does not work. It only leads to depression and imbalance. Certainly, you should have time to have fun. But keeping this discipline will help keep you in an enlightened state of awareness.

5.The final step to become enlightened is surrender. Once, through purification, shaktipat and meditation that spiritual energy current is powerfully moving through you, all that is left is surrender, to allow your experience to be as it is. To accept yourself as you are and allow yourself to feel what is here, to feel it as sensation. Although discipline is very important, you come to the point where you have to surrender trying to do enlightenment, because as said before, it is the shaktipat that awakens you to enlightenment. Once you feel the Shakti as a constant in your life, you surrender to it; you allow it to do its work. You allow yourself to dissolve into bliss.

The other way to receive shaktipat is through sound. There is some very special meditation music that emits shaktipat, so simply by listening to the music, this spiritual energy is awakened in you and helps you become enlightened. It means you can be anywhere, listening to the music on your CD player or mp3 player and the shaktipat of the music will be awakening you into bliss.

CHAPTER 3

THE TWO STAGES OF SAMADHI

Samadhi means union with God. The union of the one who has mastered Samadhi is never disturbed. The states of waking, dreaming, or sleeping are, therefore, not hindrances. The seeker remains continuously conscious that he is atman and not the body. As a big hall is seen after breaking down the walls standing between four rooms, the yogi experiences only Samadhi after the differences between the aforesaid states vanish. This is called sahajavastha (the natural state).

As such, Samadhi is only one, but it has two stages:

1. The first is called Samprajnata, Savikalpa, sabija, or cetana samadhi; the other is asamprajnata, nirvikalpa, nirbija, oracetana samadhi. The difference between these two stages is very clear. The mind exists in the first Samadhi, but not in the second.

2. The second stage can also be called atimanasa (super-mind).Bija (the seed) of all desires is the mind. Since the mind exists in the first or the lower samadhi, it is called sabija (with seed) samadhi. This state is also known as samprajnata samadhi since in it, one attains doubtless and true knowledge about the object of

concentration. It is also called prasantavahita since the prana and apana vayus, moving upward through the passage of susumna, stabilize the external organs and generate concentration of mind. Moreover, this state is also known as savikalpa samadhi or cetanasamadhi, because sankalpa (volition) and smrti (memory) do not exist in it.

Since the susumna passage of the seeker who has reached savikalpa samadhi is purified, the feeble and upward-flowing prana and apana produce physical and mental stability, further resulting in deep concentration. In common concentration, one has to make a decision, and therefore, many favorable as well as contradicting thoughts occur. But in the state of perfect concentration or samadhi a decision is reached naturally, and there are no contradicting thoughts. Meditation devoid of conflicting thoughts is called savikalpas amadhi, and meditation without either favorable or contradicting thoughts is called nirvikalpa Samadhi.

Since the mind exists in savikalpa Samadhi, 'I' exists until the end. Because of the existence of 'I', 'you' and 'they' remain also. Thus duality prevails until the end of savikalpa Samadhi. This means that as long as the seeker is in the stage of savikalpa samadhi there is still the duality jiva (soul) and Isvara (God). In nirvikalpa samadhi, mind becomes non-mind and jiva merges into Siva (God). As a result, duality disappears.

The cause of duality is the drsta (the one who sees). In the state of advaita (non-dual state) there is no drsta (seer) at all. Without mastering savikalpa Samadhi, one cannot practice nirvikalpa samadhi. Savikalpa samadhi is the base of nirvikalpa samadhi.

THE FIRST STAGE OF SAMADHI: SEPARATION OF BODY AND MIND

In savikalpa Samadhi, the body is separated from the mind and in nirvikalpa samadhi the mind is separated from the soul. Savikalpa Samadhi, which is active, is attained when deep concentration is generated through the practice of meditation in which the mind's control over the body is lifted and the senses are made introvert by means of free prana. Nirvikalpa Samadhi is the natural 'state of non-mind (or state of nothingness) which is generated thereafter. In that state, the mind merges into nature and the atman (soul) emerges as the self.

The separation of the mind from the body occurs in the first state of Samadhi. As a result, prana becomes independent and free from the control of the mind. The independent prana takes over control of the body, directs it, and tries to make the senses introvert. In this state, the seeker watches the activities of prank and the senses as a witness. Such practice is called Samkhya Yoga, Raja Yoga, or Purna Yoga.

In Samkhya Yoga, it is believed that all actions are performed through the qualities of nature; hence only nature is the 'doer'. "I" is only a pure, wise and free soul. "I" has nothing to do with the actions of nature. In the Bhagavad Gita it is said, "Oh mighty armed (Arjuna)! He who knows in essence the divisions and relations of the qualities of nature and their activities and thinks that the qualities (as sense organs) react to the qualities (as sense-propensities), is not attached."

Raja Yoga is the best form of yoga. It is also called Purna Yoga or Asamprajnata Yoga. Karma Yoga or Kriya Yoga is its integral part. Control of the physical senses is achieved by Karma Yoga and control of the subtle senses is achieved by Raja Yoga. Savikalpa samadhi is the base of Raja Yoga. Since there is only concentration in that state, the mind exists. Because of this, it is also called cetana Samadhi.

In Raja Yoga Samadhi, there is no existence of mind; hence it is called acetana Samadhi. After mastering this Samadhi, a yogi's spiritual practice comes to an end. He remains at all times in Samadhi whether he is sitting, standing, walking, eating, drinking, speaking, or doing anything else. Yet, if he desires, he can at will enter into acetana samadhi.

The Four Samapattis (States of Meditation)

There are four stages of meditation through which a seeker has to pass before reaching sabija or Samprajnata Samadhi. These stages are called savitarka (deliberative), savicara(reflective), sananda (joyful), and sasmita (self-realized) samapattis (states of meditation).The subject or object of meditation, the means or the instrument of meditation, and the doer or the mediator-these three form a trio.

Because of this trio, the samapattis are also divided into three categories. In the first category, the subject or object supporting the mind in meditation is considered important. In the second, the means or instrument of meditation is considered important, while in the third the doer or the meditator is given importance.

In meditation, the subject-object is called grahya (that which is comprehended), the means-instrument is grahana (comprehension), and the doer meditatoris grahitr (one who comprehends). In other words, they form a trio of known, knowledge, and knower. In savitarka and savicara samapattis, grahya or the subject or object of meditation is important, so both these samapattis fall under the first category.

This is based on grahya, that is, on what is known or comprehended in meditation. In sananda samapatti, grahana, or the means or instrument of meditation is important; hence it falls under the second category. Sasmita samapatti falls under the third category in which grahitr or the doer is important.

a)Savitarka Samapatti

After the release of prana, the kundalini power of the seeker is awakened. Thereafter begins savitarka samapatti, or the deliberative state of meditation. In this state, the mind is directed towards its supporting object, yielding gross direct experience. Here the mental concentration assumes the form of deliberation.

Because of the sense organs, the mind constantly remains extroverted. Therefore, first of all it should be applied or focused on gross objects. Such gross objects, which may support the mind for the deliberation during meditation, can be five major gross elements (viz. earth, water, fire, air, and ether) or the gross forms of God (Brahma,Visnu, Siva, etc.). Thus a sort of dharana (focusing of mind) begins during savitarka samapatti.

This samapatti is further divided into two types: savitarkanugata andnirvitarkanugata. During savitarkanugata samapatti there is gross direct experience of the supporting object along with the deliberation of the mind. On the other hand, innirvitarkanugata samapatti there is gross direct experience of the supporting object without deliberation.

During savitarka samapatti, the mind of the seeker remains, perturbed. After the release of prana, as the seeker advances in the practice of meditation, he confronts certain yogic experiences which frighten him. He is unable to make the right decision at this stage about the validity of such disturbing or troublesome experiences. Therefore, this stage corresponds with the ksiptavastha (the mental state of distraction) in meditation.

b) Savicara Samapatti

After transcending the state of savitarka samapatti, the seeker gives up the gross form of meditation and adopts the subtle form. With that change he enters into the next stage of savicara samapatti: In this state of meditation, the mind is directed towards its supporting subject, yielding subtle direct experience. Here, the mind reflects upon the subtle subjects of meditation. In the initial stage of meditation, there is a need for gross subjects to support the mind in its contemplative efforts, but later on it can easily reflect upon even subtle supporting subjects.

Among such subtle subjects to support the reflection of the mind during meditation can be included the five basic subtle elements: sabda (hearing), sparsa (touch), rupa (sight), rasa (taste), and gandha (smell). Savicara samapatti is also further divided into two types: savicaranugata and nirvicaranugata. In the first type, experience is supported by the reflection of the mind, while in the second type there is subtle experience without the support of reflection.

During savicara samapatti, the seeker is still not able to find the right explanation or solution for the troublesome experiences which he undergoes right from the stage of savitarka samapatti.

So he is still in a state of uncertainty and still finds total darkness spread over his path. He is quite stupefied, due to his inability to solve the problem. However, he tries to compromise by believing that in spite of all the disturbing experiences, it is continuous practice that will lead him to the goal. This stage corresponds with the mudhavastha (the mental state of stupefaction) in meditation.

c) Sananda Samapatti

When the seeker progresses further and transcends the first two samapattis, his support of the subject or the object of meditation is automatically done away with. Subsequently, he enters sananda samapatti in which meditation is supported by means of the sense organs. Since grahana (comprehension) is accomplished through the sense organs, during sananda samapatti, meditation is automatically focused on them, giving joyful feelings to the seeker.

The mental states of distraction and stupefaction vanish during this samapatti and the seeker feels inner happiness. This stage corresponds with the viksiptavastha (the mental state of serenity) in meditation. Concentration of mind, which has eluded the seeker so far, occurs to them sporadically. Such stray glimpses of concentration of mind generate rays of hope in the seeker of the possibility of reaching their goal. Thus they experience happiness and joy and their mind remains calm.

(d) Sasmiti Samapatti

After transcending the stage of sananda samapatti, when the seeker enters the fourth or sasmita samapatti, their meditation is not supported by the sense organs but by the sense of personality. In this stage, the seeker meditates on the 'self', and grahitr (the mediator) is important, leaving aside all subjects, objects, or means of supporting the mind.

37

This is the stage of self-realization or sabija, savikalpa, samprajnata or cetanasamadhi, in which the mind attains real concentration.

In the first three samapattis, the mind remains either perturbed or joyful but lacks perfect concentration. Therefore, these are not included in the state of samadhi. Since they are lower states as compared to Samadhi, they are called samapattis. They can be considered immature states of Samadhi. But the last, or sasmita samapatti, yields perfect concentration of mind, true knowledge and bliss. Hence it is a state mature enough to be identified as Samadhi.

Samapattis, Qualities of Nature, and the Sense of Non-Attachment

Like samapattis, the sense of non-attachment is also attained stage by stage. Broadly speaking, there are two levels of non-attachment: apara vairagya (lower category of nonattachment) and para vairagya (higher category). Apara vairagya is further divided into four stages:

1) Yatamana vairagya,

2) Vyatireka vairagya,

3) Ekendriya vairagya, and

4) Vasikara vairagya.

All these four types of non-attachment are related to the four stages of samapatti.

During savitarka samapatti, the seeker has many physical and mental impurities. As a result, rajas and tamas become predominant and sattva remains subsidiary or dormant in the seeker. However, the seeker decides to get rid of the impurities through spiritual practice and strives for this. These sincere efforts to overcome the impurities and the lower qualities of nature give them a sense of non-attachment called yatamana vairagya.

In the next stage of savicara samapatti, the fleeting nature of the mind is somewhat reduced due to partial removal of the physical and mental impurities. The physical activity is also reduced. Therefore, the seeker finds some solace and develops the patience to persevere in spiritual practice. Such a state gives the seeker a sense of nonattachment called vyatireka vairagya.

During the stage of sananda samapatti, rajas and tamas are somewhat reduced in the seeker, allowing sattva to develop. As a result, the restless mind becomes serene and the body becomes purified and healthy. Sense objects do not attract the attention, as compared to the earlier stages. In this stage, one attains the sense of non-attachment called ekendriya vairagya.

Finally, in sasmita samapatti, both rajas and tamas fade away and sattva becomes dominant. This sattva lends stability to the mind and the body, removing the impurities. Mental bliss and true knowledge attained during this samapatti give the seeker a sense of non-attachment called vasikara vairagya. This vasikara itself is the real apara vairagya. However, para vairagya (highest non-attachment) can only be attained through nirbija, nirvikalpa, asamprajnata or acetana samadhi.

Ups and Downs in the Mental State during Samapatti

In the state of savitarka samapatti, the seeker is in a very distracted state. In savicara samapatti, distraction is replaced by a stupefied state of mind. In sananda samapatti, one mistakenly considers himself to be a great or mahayogi, and as a result, tries to falsify the yoga teachings of preceding teachers. He plans many big schemes and pretends that siddhis have become his slave. In this state, he continuously dreams of siddhis. In sasmita samapatti, as tamoguna and rajoguna are annihilated, sattvaguna develops and he begins to see his mistakes. Then he likes being alone, dislikes public contact, and feels more interested in the deep study of the scriptures.

A seeker has to swim a stormy ocean from savitarka to sasmita samadhi. During that period, he experiences joy and depression over and over again. When a seeker has divine experiences, he becomes overjoyed and feels very enthusiastic, but these excessive feelings often invite contradictory thoughts. As a result, he considers untruth to be truth.

When he has such divine experiences in the state of excessive perturbance, he takes truth to be untruth. Thus he is often led astray. Savitarka, savicara, sananda and sasmita--these four samapattis are linked one to the other. Because of this, even when a seeker suddenly climbs to a higher samapatti from a lower one, he is led astray and thinks 'now samadhi is within my grasp.' When this experience does not last, he becomes disheartened. The more he has such experiences, the less impact joy as well as depression has on his mind.

Finally, he reaches the safe bank of sasmita samapatti and becomes completely free from the impact of joy and depression. This is because he begins to attain the higher wisdom in this state. In spite of this, the detachment generated in his mind at this stage is called apara vairagya (incomplete detachment, also known as vasikaravairagya). Asamprajnata samadhi can be mastered only after attaining para vairagya (complete detachment), which considers even the power of omniscience to be a trifle, and enables the seeker to go forward.

Pratyahara through the Samapattis

In savikaipa Samadhi, there is mere concentration. In that state, since prana and apana have become subtle and strong, the seeker can enter samadhi whenever and wherever he chooses. Even a seeker receiving saktipata diksa, in spite of being a beginner, can begin meditation whenever and wherever he chooses. But that meditation is just the beginning of samapatti and is of a much lower order compared to savikalpa samadhi.

The beginning of samapatti can be called the beginning of pratyahara. If asana and pranayama are considered the first two stages of yoga, pratyahara becomes the third stage, while samadhi will be the sixth. In the second stage, (pranayama), pratyahara is very weak, but when the seeker is well established in the third stage (pratyahara), pranayama is at its best.

As a result, kumbhaka (withholding of the breath) lasts longer and the nadis, (bodily passages) cakras and grant his are speedily purified. As they are relieved of impurities, the body becomes more and more stable, in other words, the senses become introvert. At that time, distraction decreases, mudhavastha (the state of stupefaction) vanishes, and viksiptavastha (the state of serenity) begins to appear.

In sananda samapatti, the yogi conquers bindu (sexual fluid) and gets the invaluable opportunity of sipping the nectar. When this state is created, it can be said that pratyahara has become stronger. Yet, there is not complete concentration (ekagrata) in this stage. When a yogi begins to climb the stage of sasmita samapatti, he attains it and feels that his hard penance for long years has yielded results.

In this stage, dharana, dhyana, and samadhi, which altogether are called samyama in Patanjali's Yogadarsana, is slowly being mastered. As a result, the stage of pratyahara vanishes forever. Khecari mudra becomes stronger and yoni mudra begins to occur. In this stage, one also comes to know what is called sambhavi mudra.

When the seeker reaches the end of the fourth, or sasmita samapatti, his mind, devoid of doubts and alternatives, becomes so steadfast that no fresh thoughts are generated. From this point begins asamprajnata or nirvikalpa samadhi. The thoughtless state begins where concentration or single-mindedness ends.

THE SECOND STATE OF SAMADHI: DISSOLUTION OF MIND

Only after mastering the first (savikalpa) samadhi can the second one, nirvikalpa Samadhi, be practiced. Even though savikalpa samadhi is considered very important, it is insignificant compared to nirvikalpa samadhi. Sage Pantanjali says, "Even the best samyama (self-control), i.e. savikalpa samadhi, is considered an external dimension of nirbija or nirvikalpa samadhi. The reason for this is that in savikalpa samadhi, the mind does not dissolve itself into the atman or the self."

It is true that rtambhara prajna (the highest wisdom) is attained through sabija, samprajnata or savikalpa samadhi or samyama, but in this samadhi there is only deep concentration and total dissolution of the mind does not occur. Therefore, a seeker must not stop after attaining rtambhara prajna. Sage Patanjali says, "After the dissolution of the mind, everything gets dissolved, and thereafter dawns nirbija or nirvikalpa Samadhi."

In that case what is the nature of nirvikalpa samadhi? The Hatha Yoga Pradipika says,

"A yogi seated in samadhi does not know (or is not conscious of) sound, touch, form, taste, and smell. He also does not differentiate between himself and others."

"As the wood supply is exhausted, the fire is extinguished in its place of origin. Similarly, as thoughts vanish, the mind also gets automatically dissolved into its source (nature)."

Since this path of yogic meditation is very difficult and full of so many obstacles, rarely does a bold and genuine aspirant reach the highest peak of savikalpa samadhi Accomplishment of nirvikalpa samadhi is ten million times more difficult than chewing an iron gram. In Mahopanisad, it is said, 'O Brahmin! To conquer the mind is more difficult than even drinking an ocean, uprooting a great mountain, or swallowing fire."

The fort of the physical body is to be conquered by savikalpa samadhi, while the fort of the mind is to be reduced by nirvikalpa samadhi. In Dhyanabindu Upanisad it is said,

"So long as the mind is not finally dissolved, it should be controlled by the heart. Only this much is real knowledge; all else is the elaboration of books."

CHAPTER 4
ABOUT TAI CHI

Chinese martial arts have a long history and possess many schools and styles. Tai Chi is one of the exquisite works of Chinese martial arts and is deeply loved by all for its positive effects in health preservation and self-defense. It is becoming more and more popular in the world with each passing day.

It is suitable for almost anyone. Tai C hi is the martial arts that can be trained and practiced by all, man or woman, old and young, sick and healthy. A constant correct practice of Tai Chi will do great help for internal organs, brains, nerves and limbs; will calm the mind and balance ourselves against the tension of the speedy modern social life.

One who practices Tai Chi will find that every movement of the routines is so naturally structured and the internal energy flow all over the body; will find it is deeply implied with ancient Chinese philosophy, producing the union of the individual soul with the universal spirit. It is one of the superior Chinese arts. A correct understanding in this theory and correct practice will offer one an everlasting happy mind, high spirit, more patience, strong will and a nicer way to grow healthy relationships with people around, which will lead anyone to a great success who obtains all these above.

Concentrating on correct posture and breathing control, Tai Chi's movements are fluid, graceful and well balanced, promoting the complete harmony of body and mind. Tai Chi provides the mental relaxation and physical fitness so essential in our modern stress-filled lives.

Because of Tai Chi comes from kung fu, every movement has a real good self defense meaning. Try it. It will give you more charisma and you will be well-balanced.

Tai Chi is an unusual form of martial arts whereby we believe in building strength, mental and physical from within, softness is stronger than hardness, moving in a curve is better than a straight line, yielding is more efficient than confronting. It is especially different from western types of sports such as rugby where the harder and quicker the better. Tai Chi is a sport that strengthens the body as well as the mind from within.

The movements of Tai Chi have the characteristics of alternating Yin with Yang that is the two opposing principles in nature, the former feminine and the later masculine, hard force with soft force, quick movements with slow ones. It also features the integration of body and spirit, the combination of internal and external cultivation. The internal cultivation includes ethical improvement and the training of inner strength. It always emphasizes the integration of morality and martial arts, giving top priority to morality.

Tai Chi - Stages of Development

In general terms, there are three stages of development of your tai chi practice.

-
- Stage One- practices your external movements so that they are done with correct posture, pacing, and direction of vision.

- Stage Two- practice how force is stored and delivered in each form.

- Stage Three- practice moving your qi to where you are delivering force.

STAGE ONE

It is important to practice your form at this stage until the movements and postures are automatic. This is the easiest stage to learn, but it can be very frustrating for beginners. Everyone else, teachers, videos, etc., seem so fluid and graceful. It takes time to get past the negative self image and learn to enjoy the movement.

Most teachers and videos do a pretty good job of explaining the movements of a tai chi form or set. However, there are many subtleties that can only be learned from a teacher. If you have access to a good teacher, great. Enjoy it and learn lots.

If you do not, do the best you can with videos, books, and other resources. Choose a common form so that you can find an occasional workshop. I recommend either the Yang 24 (Beijing) forms or the Tai Chi for Arthritis from Dr. Paul Lam Tai Chi for Health Community. There are many good weekend workshops available.

There are a few simple things that you should know as you begin your practice. Take your time and learn methodically. Learning faster is not necessarily better. Work through learning the forms at a steady pace and take your time in understanding the details. It's better to learn a few forms or sets well than lots of them carelessly. Plan on learning only 1 or 2 new forms each week.

Remember the 70% rule. Estimate your greatest ability to perform an exercise. Practice at only 70% of that level. This is not a competition. If it hurts, stop immediately. Apply this rule to everything in tai chi, from how far you stretch, to how many repetitions, and to how long you practice. As you become more familiar with the forms and with your own body, you can gradually increase this.

A good first principle at this stage is to learn control of your movements so they are slow, smooth, and continuous. You should move as though there is a gentle resistance. Think of your qi flow as a river. As it flows downhill, it gathers strength. Keep your movements slow, smooth, and continuous to smooth the progress of the qi flow.

Another way to think about controlling your movements is to work on body alignment. Being upright is very important, but it is not as simple as it seems. A way to approach it is to think of your spine as a string. Imagine gently stretching the string from both ends. Being upright provides the internal organs with more space. An upright body also strengthens the internal deep stabilizer muscles. Try to keep your body upright and supple throughout all the movements. Be especially aware of this when you start bending your knees because your alignment can change. When you bend your knees, imagine that you are sitting down in a straight chair (not the Lazy Boy!) and keep your back fairly straight. Use a mirror or video camera to check yourself while practicing.

Practice a little each day. Ten minutes of practice each day will bring you better results than practicing for an hour at a time once a week. You will find that tai chi is more challenging than it looks. If you need a break, take one. Frequently, take time to review what you have learned.

Summary of Stage One

Work on your form and posture. Start to learn the essential principles of Tai chi. Read Yang Chen Fu's Ten Essential Principles and start to incorporate them into your practice. Most of them won't make much sense yet, but that's OK. Keep returning to them and it will become more clear in time.

STAGE TWO

In stage two, study each form in detail and understand the details. Most of my experience in is Yang style, so this explanation will follow that experience.

Even the simplest forms have several (many) parts to learn and master. It is a big oversimplification, but we can say that the six things to focus on at this point are 1) what your feet are doing, 2) what your hands are doing, 3) what your waist (body) is doing, 4) what your eyes are doing, 5) opening, and 6) closing.

According to the classics of tai chi, "Internal force is rooted in the feet, developed by the legs, governed by the waist, and expressed in the hands." This internal force is a spiral force generated at the feet that causes the waist to rotate, which leads the hands in the various tai chi forms. Spiral force is beyond the scope of this article, but the comments about the feet, waist, and hands are important at this point in your learning.

1) What is your stance? What are your feet doing? There are many stationary stances, from horse stance with equal weighting on each foot (wu ji); to bow stance, with the 70/30 weight ratio (brush knee); to empty stance, where essentially all your weight is on one leg (playing lute); and T stance during transitions (fair lady works shuttles). In addition, you should become familiar with dropping stance (snake creeps down) and independent stance (golden rooster stands on one leg). Other forms have stances that I am not familiar with, such as sitting stance, pan knee stance, and cross stance. The stance is important in delivering force (power) during each form.

2) Your hands should be in certain places during the movements of the form. Your hands deliver force during each form. Understand this and be aware of it during each form. There are many specific hand positions and shapes for different forms. I'll write about that someday.

3) The waist is the part of the body above the hip bones and below the diaphragm. The waist can be moved independently of the hips in some forms. In general, most forms have turning movements. The waist should lead the movement of the arms and the rest of the body. This increases/improves the delivery of force.

4) During most forms, your eyes should follow your hand(s) during movement. When your hands are moving separately, your eyes should follow the dominant hand. The dominant hand is the one that is delivering force. This is usually the higher hand or the one that is the most forward. For example, during brush knee, the hand that pushes forward is dominant and should be followed with your eyes. The hand that brushes the knee is not dominant. However, this statement is a little misleading. Your eyes really should be looking "through" your hand at a point beyond the hands to where you want your force to be delivered.

5) Every form has an open. This is the part of the form where power is developed and stored. Think of it as a bow and arrow. Pulling on the bowstring is opening and storing energy. For example, during brush knee, one hand goes back while the other one is placed somewhere near your elbow. This is the opening where you are storing energy.

In general, you should inhale sometime during opening movements. Chen Jin, a Chen-style tai chi master, wrote that when you are opening, you are solid outside and soft inside. You can feel your body soften as you inhale and expand your abdomen.

6) Every form has a close. This is the part of the form where power is delivered. Again, think of it as a bow and arrow. Releasing the bow

string is closing and delivering energy. For example, during brush knee, one hand goes forward while the other one brushes past your knee. This is the closing where you are delivering energy.

In general, you should exhale sometime during closing movements. Chen Jin, a Chen-style tai chi master, wrote that when you are closing, you are soft outside and solid inside. You can feel your inside harden, or become more solid, when you are delivering force as you contract your abdomen.

Summary of Stage 2

Continue to learn the essential principles of tai chi. Read Yang Chen Fu's Ten Essential Principles and start to incorporate them into your practice. They should be starting to make more sense now. Keep returning to them and it will become clearer in time.

STAGE THREE

In stage three, you begin to learn to use your intent to direct the flow of qi through your body. Mental focus is essential to this step.

Circulating Your Qi

The next phase of understanding open and close (see Stage 2 for more information) is to start moving your qi as you open and close. When you open (inhale), move your qi from your dan tien, through your perineum, and up your yang meridian (along your spine) toward the bai hui point at the crown of your head. When you close (exhale), move your qi down your yin meridian (the front center of your body) to the lower dan tien.

Keep your mouth gently closed with your tongue touching your upper palate. It may take a long time (years) to become comfortable with this. It is important that you do not force your breathing here. If you are not sure where to be inhaling and exhaling or you get tired, just allow your body to breathe naturally.

Intent

There is a statement in the tai chi classics that says something like, "The mind (intent) moves the internal energy and the internal energy moves the body." This is an important principle, but it is difficult to learn. It is important to practice your way through the three stages of development before you can really understand intent.

"Whenever the "use of intent" is mentioned with regard to the practice of Taijiquan, most Taijiquan practitioners think 'the mind is the primary controller and the body is the follower. This is illustrated in Yang

Cheng Fu's Ten Essential Principles of Taijiquanas "use intent, not muscular strength.'

There are usually three meanings of intent when discussed in Taijiquan. The first meaning is 'to pay attention to one's internal strength." The second meaning of intent is the same as the term "internal energy' or qi. For example, 'the movement of the intent' or 'the intention (qi) must change with vigor while remaining circular and smooth.' The third meaning of intent is 'expectations' or 'thoughts.' "

The emphasis on intent is important in tai chi because the use of strength is very different than other martial arts. Tai chi uses slow, soft force to deflect or divert an opponent's energy instead of meeting force with force. This allows time for your mind to contemplate the movement and imagine the movement in your mind before your muscles actually moves.

When you are practicing tai chi, move slowly and continuously and use intent to move beyond the physical part of the form. This helps to develop a strong mind-body connection. Qi gets stronger as it continues to flow, just like the force of water gets stronger as it flows downhill. If you stop moving during the forms, your qi also stops moving.

Intent also involves the use of your eyes. In the tai chi classics, it says something like, "The eyes and the hands must follow each other."

However, this does not mean that your eyes must exactly follow the movement of your hands. It means that your eyes and hands must arrive at the same point at the same time.

Don't forget that tai chi is an internal art. This means that the movements begin in your mind. Your intention leads the movements of your energy. And from that energy, you create an internal force. As you move, think about applying a soft gentle force to your movements. Use that to lead your movements. Eventually, you will begin to feel the internal energy move within you. The key is to practice regularly.

TAI CHI - WHAT IT CAN DO FOR YOU

Tai Chi - you may have heard of it but do really know the meaning behind the term? The term Tai Chi, literally translated as "Supreme Ultimate Force", is a well-known ancient martial arts originated in China. It aims to transform an individual into a state of infinite and absolute potential - a concept that conforms to the age-old Chinese philosophy of Yin and Yang. Moreover, the term Tai Chi also denotes "unity, one, or being able to attain oneness."

Although a martial art, it is different from other conventional forms of martial arts. It may have forms or sets consisting of many sequential movements derived from martial arts, but the manner in which these are performed can be likened to the gracefulness of meditating in Yoga. So, instead of explosive kicks and hard-core punches, it utilizes force expressed it in a graceful, efficient, and invigorating way.

Over the years, the popularity of Tai Chi has increased and it is practiced in many parts of the world including the West. The reason behind its popularity is due to the health benefits it can bring to a person. Practitioners perceive the art as a form of meditative interaction between the mind, body, soul and the surroundings. Many practitioners discover its primary benefit may not just be for martial self defense, but as an exercise to promote wellness and balance.

Now, with respect to Chinese medicine and philosophy, it is believed that the "Chi" or life energy is essential to the overall vitality of the body. When Tai Chi is practiced, it creates an energy flow that will circulate throughout the entire body and enhance the well-being of a person. Once the "chi" circulates around the body, it goes to the pattern of the vascular and nervous system and any organ correlated to it. This is why the art is often connected to the principle of traditional Chinese healing and acupuncture.

Practitioners have proved numerous health benefits of the art. Among the benefits they have acquired are improved blood circulation, correct posture, healthy vital organs and good digestion. With practice their muscle tone and strength increased, their balance and coordination improved. And Tai Chi does not just provide physical benefits; it also enhances the mind and the spirit. Tai Chi teaches you how to focus, so that mind and body energy works together as one. When practicing, people find that they are not just more physically fit but, happier, and vigorous as well.

It is this harnessing of mental and physical energy that makes Tai Chi not just any form of martial arts but an exercise that helps you cultivate the highest level of physical, mental and spiritual development.

TAI CHI FOR SPORTS

Tai Chi is awesome as a sports training tool because its goal is to cultivate balance, calm and power. Those are three things one needs to excel in any physical activity. During Tai Chi practice you learn about the lower dan tien, which is an energy center located just below the navel. Tai Chi players are taught to move from their dan tien, which is their center of gravity. This is especially helpful for skateboarding, snowboarding, surfing and skiing. Likewise, in baseball, golf, tennis and racquetball you swing from the center, or dan tien, to hit the ball.

Let's take baseball for example: Tai Chi's ability to improve balance is excellent for infielders, who move and reach quickly and sharply. And just before going into a pitch, a pitcher must hold his/her balance on one leg for several seconds. This point of balance can determine the force and accuracy of the pitch.

The concept of swinging from the dan tien may also help reduce "golfer's back" because by creating the swing from below the navel there is less twisting of the lower back. This relaxed motion allows the entire force of the dan tien's turning to be projected outward through the hands and club into the ball. Many golfers discover that they can drive the ball much farther after practicing Tai Chi for only a few months.

The same force used in golf also works for tennis and racquetball. In addition, consciously moving from the dan tien can lessen the pressure on the knees, especially through all the quick stops of the game.

Of course, the mental acuity, balance and self-esteem Tai Chi encourages are beneficial for other types of sports as well, such as football and soccer. It is well known that the L.A. Lakers basketball team used Tai Chi as part of their training.

ESSENTIAL IDEAS OF TAI CHI

Training Tai Chi isn't simply a swing with the arm and also the movement of the feet. There is a reason behind each movement and fashion that's made. These ideas paved the way to constructing every type of Tai Chi. So you have to spend close attention on the issues that are not introduced up every once in a while because even though if things appear so fundamental, they're certainly essential.

Here are 10 of probably the most important concepts of Tai Chi that you ought to never take for granted. Keep in mind these and it'll make you appreciate more the types that are performed.

Concept #1

Tai Chi is done with emphasis on each motion and also the fashion of every sample must be in linked with one an additional. Which means each motion made must always begin from the spine, heading lower to the waist, then moving lower to the legs and theft, then it's concurrently heading up to the body then the arms, hands and last, the fingers.

Concept #2

Preserve your shoulders dropped so that any tension will be eliminated. Shoulders that are usually propped are stated to have overflowing tension.

Idea #3

Your wrists should be straight in buy to type a lady's palm if you're carrying out the Cheng form. All factors apply to all types of Tai Chi but the lady's hand is basic and a very essential trait with the Cheng type in buy to cultivate the power flowing within the body.

Concept #4

Shifting slowly ought to always be done every step of the way in which in which. It might never be overemphasized because the slow smoothness of one's motions will improve the connection of one's physique as well as your atmosphere.

Idea #5

Never let anything disconnect you. You ought to usually remain connected with every instruction. If you have been disconnected, carry on to perform the actions and listen carefully towards the instructions so that you can overcome any distraction.

Concept #6

Your knees must usually be bent throughout the whole form. Your height must not bob down and up. You will find some concerns but all the although, your height should be maintained at a level that's continuous.

Idea #7

The energy of Tai Chi travels differently in the movement of Tai Chi. Energy of Tai Chi will start in the ft going up to the legs, controlling the shoulders, and will be expressed by the fingers and fingers.

Concept #8

Your head should be taken care of as if it was suspended on air.

Idea #9

Your chest must be depressed and your back again should be raised but this should be done without exerting any drive.

Idea #10

Your breath should be focused on your dan-tien but force should not be exerted. As time in the program may pass, there will probably be accomplishments which will fulfill you want synchronizing your breathing with the actions that you simply make.

You should usually seek advice from your instructor when to exhale or inhale.

CHAPTER 5

PEAK PERFORMANCE: HOW TO GET "INTO THE ZONE"

Many people associate peak performance with sports and the arts, and that's where its roots are found. When athletes and performers are in "the zone," a state achieved by operating at peak performance, they are completely at one with what they're doing and able to control their destiny-at least for a moment.

The idea of getting into the zone isn't limited to those who operate on a big stage. You need the following seven essential elements to experience peak performance:

- Strike a balance between the challenges you face and your skills.
- Have total absorption and concentration on the tasks required-be completely focused.
- Receive unambiguous feedback on the process.
- Realize a sense of control or confidence in yourself/your vision.
- Feel intrinsically rewarded.
- Experience a transformation of time.
- Identify clear and specific goals.

Moving beyond your comfort zone is an important first step. It might sound counterintuitive, but you have to challenge yourself-and even become uncomfortable-to be able to experience the benefit of being in the zone. Challenge actually leads to flow, an important peak performance determinant.

Being fully engaged, making continual adjustments based on your instincts and objective data, and combating self-doubt with positive statements are other behaviors that will put you on the track to peak performance and being in the zone.

All your efforts can go for naught unless you know where you're going-but you must not forget to focus on the process it takes to get you there. When you're immersed in something, it's often effortless, and time seems to fly by. This is called being in the moment and it takes nothing away from the end result, but is an important step toward achieving it.

What does your successful future look like? The answer is going to be different for everyone, thus it can add significant value to your peak performance journey to develop a strategic plan as well as a support system to help keep you on track to achieving your goals.

As part of your strategic plan, you should:

- Create a personal mission statement
- Identify outcome goals (production/assets under management)
- Identify specific behavioral process goals that will lead to your outcome goals
- Break down your goals into doable steps
- Identify and commit to different activities and establish the priority you believe they should have

While you might not be focused on winning the World Series or taking home an Academy Award, you can learn from the process famed athletes and performers have used to achieve those goals. Set your sights on becoming a peak performer and working in the zone in your arena.

PREVENTS PEAK PERFORMANCE IN SPORTS

Athletes tend to assume or believe that with hard training, getting into great physical condition and practicing their techniques for thousands of time it will enable them to achieve and maintain peak performance in sports.

Although the above actions will certainly help you it won't enable you to have control over the level of performance for the following reasons:

1. Although almost all athletes will agree they need to have great timing in their training and in competition they don't know how to apply this timing training in their sport.

2. Athletes' speed training is only done on the physical side and should be done through the mind first.

3. The tempo or flow of the game is an area that athletes and coaches have no clue about and will prevent them from being able to control the play or game into their advantage.

4. Athletes usually have problems with their reflex actions in which they'll either freeze up in their movements or be too soon or too late in the execution.

5. Athletes have problems with balance, power and the overall reach and distance in their performance because they lack the knowledge on how to use their body mechanics to elite levels.

6. Athletes tend to not know about the importance of breathing in their sport that prevents them from achieving peak levels of energy and the overall physical performance.

7. Athletes have a lack of knowledge on how to achieve and maintain the correct mental focus to enable them to control their fears, doubts, phobias and self sabotage.

There are millions of athletes in all sports that have the above problems, frustrations and concerns and desperately want to solve these things in their sport.

The big problem comes into play because there isn't anybody that can advise them on how to overcome these problems.

There have been some major developments and information that could help any athletes and maybe you should check things out for yourself and you can be the judge.

Printed in Great Britain
by Amazon

78722238R00047